Games Around the World

Marbles

by Elizabeth Dana Jaffe

Content Adviser: Professor Sherry L. Field, Department of Social Science Education, College of Education, The University of Georgia

Reading Adviser: Dr. Linda D. Labbo, Department of Reading Education, College of Education, The University of Georgia

COMPASS POINT BOOKS
MINNEAPOLIS, MINNESOTA

Compass Point Books
3722 West 50th Street, #115
Minneapolis, MN 55410

Visit Compass Point Books on the Internet at *www.compasspointbooks.com* or e-mail your request to *custserv@compasspointbooks.com*

Editors: E. Russell Primm and Emily J. Dolbear
Photo Researcher: Svetlana Zhurkina
Photo Selector: Linda S. Koutris
Designer: Bradfordesign, Inc.
Illustrator: Abby Bradford

Library of Congress Cataloging-in-Publication Data

Jaffe, Elizabeth D.
    Marbles / by Elizabeth Dana Jaffe ; content adviser, Sherry L. Field ; reading adviser, Linda D. Labbo.
        p. cm. — (Games around the world)
    Includes bibliographical references and index.
    ISBN 0-7565-0135-0 (hardcover : lib. bdg.)
        1. Marbles (Game)—Juvenile literature. [1. Marbles (Game) 2. Games.] I. Field, Sherry L. II. Labbo, Linda D. III. Title.
    GV1213 .J34 2002
    796.2—dc21   2001001594

Table of Contents

Do You Want to Be a Mibster?

Do you know what **shooters** and **mibs** are? They are small balls. They are usually made of glass. They can be beautiful colors. They often have swirls in them. Can you guess now? They are marbles!

You can shoot, roll, drop, or toss marbles. You can play marbles inside or outside. You need a level surface. You can play on the dirt or on a smooth floor.

People all over the world play marbles for fun. Some people also play marbles in organized matches. If you work at it, you could become a **mibster**. A mibster is a master marble player.

▲ *Marbles come in many sizes and colors.*

◄ *Children play marbles in the streets of Indonesia.*

The History of Marbles

Children and adults have played marbles for a long time. People in ancient Rome and Egypt played marbles more than 3,000 years ago. When the Romans took over other countries, they brought their marbles with them. In this way, people in other parts of the world learned to play marbles.

In the past, people used peas, beans, and nuts as marbles. They also used small stones or bits of clay.

In 1846, someone thought of a new way to make marbles. In Germany, Johann Greiner invented special scissors. These

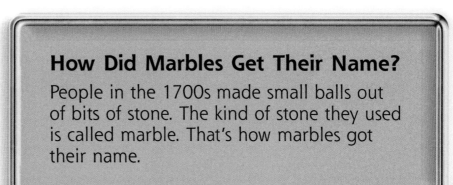

How Did Marbles Get Their Name?

People in the 1700s made small balls out of bits of stone. The kind of stone they used is called marble. That's how marbles got their name.

◄ *A marble game in the mid-1800s*

scissors cut off bits of melted glass and shaped them into balls. Those balls were marbles!

In the 1890s, machines began making glass marbles. These marbles cost less, and more people could afford them.

In 1902, an American named Martin F. Christensen built an even better machine. This machine made marbles very quickly and very cheaply.

Today, some people still make beautiful marbles by hand. But most of the marbles people buy today are made by machines. People around the world buy 5 billion marbles a year.

▲ *Boys playing marbles about 1900*

Ways to Shoot Marbles

There are many ways to shoot marbles. The way you shoot depends on the game you are playing. It also depends on the surface you are playing on. You can play marbles on smooth or uneven surfaces.

▲ *Place the marble on your thumbnail.*

On smooth sidewalks and floors, you can shoot a marble by **fulking**. First, curl up all your fingers. Then rest your marble in your curled forefinger. (That's the finger next to your thumb.) Put your thumbnail behind the marble. Kneel and bend over. Then aim and flick your thumb to shoot the marble. You don't need to keep your shooting hand on the ground.

▲ *Then shoot!*

Fulking is the most common way to shoot a marble. ▶

Knuckling down gives you better aim than fulking. The only difference is that you rest the knuckle of your forefinger on the ground. Then flick your thumb to shoot the marble. Most mibsters shoot this way.

On uneven grass and thick carpets, you may shoot in other ways. You may drop, toss, or roll your shooter.

▲ *Rest your knuckle on the ground.*

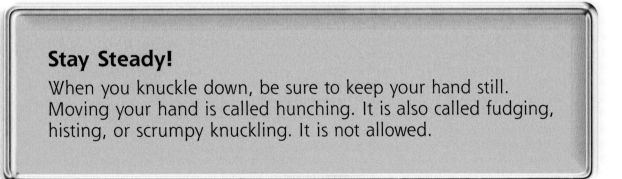

Stay Steady!

When you knuckle down, be sure to keep your hand still. Moving your hand is called hunching. It is also called fudging, histing, or scrumpy knuckling. It is not allowed.

◀ *Knuckling down*

Bombsies is a way to shoot by standing over the target marble. You hold the shooter just below eye level. Then you drop the shooter on the target marble.

Lofting is a way to make your shooter fly through the air before it hits the ground. **Bowling** is when you throw your shooter underhand or roll it on the ground.

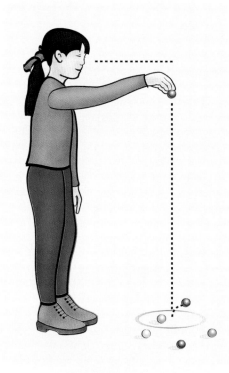

▲ *Bombsies*

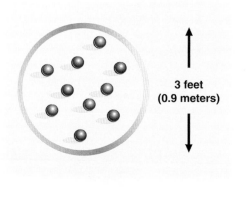

3 feet
(0.9 meters)

◄ *In bombsies, each player puts five marbles in the circle.*

You can use a **span shot** on both smooth and uneven surfaces. A **span** is the distance between the full reach of your thumb and any other finger on the same hand.

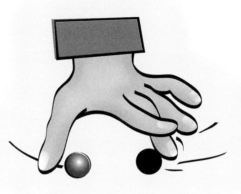

▲ *A span shot*

If your shooter and the target marble are within a span of each other, you can take a span shot.

You put your thumb outside one marble and the other finger outside the other marble. Snap your finger and thumb to knock the marbles together.

▲ *A span*

15

Basic Marble Games

You can set up marble games in many ways. You can set them up with circles, triangles, and squares. You can also use hoops, holes, strings, or boxes. For games outside, you can mark the ground with chalk. For games inside, you can use masking tape or thread.

The marble you shoot with is called the shooter marble, or the shooter. It is also called the **taw**. The marble you try to hit is called a mib. The taw is usually bigger than the mib.

In most marble games, you try to hit mibs with your shooter. Or you try to get your shooter into a hole or through a hoop.

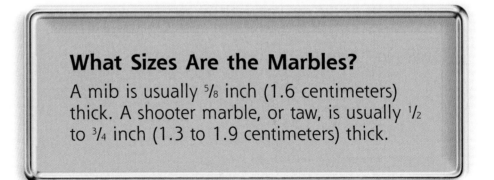

What Sizes Are the Marbles?

A mib is usually 5/8 inch (1.6 centimeters) thick. A shooter marble, or taw, is usually 1/2 to 3/4 inch (1.3 to 1.9 centimeters) thick.

◄ *You chalk a circle on the ground to play some marble games.*

Lagging—Who Goes First?

Before you start any marble game, you have to decide who plays first. You can play a shooting game called **lagging** to decide. This game is played around the world.

Number of players:	Two or more
Setup:	Draw two lines on the ground about 10 feet (3 meters) apart. The line you shoot from is called the **taw line**.
How to shoot:	However you choose
Object:	To shoot your marble closest to the other line without crossing it
How to play:	
1.	Players stand behind one line and shoot their marble towards the other line.

2. The winner is the player whose marble lands closest to the line without crossing it. If a player's marble lands on the line, that player wins.

3. Remember, the winner in a game of lagging is the first player in a marble game. (The other players follow according to how close their marbles were to the line.)

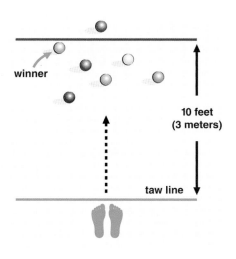

winner

10 feet
(3 meters)

taw line

▲ The player whose marble lands closest to the line without crossing it wins.

▲ Lagging

Ringtaw—A Game from the United States

People in the United States have played ringtaw for more than 100 years. You use circles to play ringtaw.

Number of players:	Two or more
Setup:	Draw a circle, or ring, 7 feet (2 meters) wide on the ground and then draw another circle 1 foot (30 centimeters) wide inside it
How to shoot:	Fulking or knuckling down
Object:	To knock the most marbles out of the inside circle
How to play:	

1. All players put the same number of mibs in the smaller circle.

2. Players shoot one at a time. From outside the bigger

circle, the first player shoots a marble at the mibs in the small circle.

3. If the player knocks a mib out of the small circle, he or she keeps the mib and plays again. This time, the player must shoot from where his or her marble landed. If the player doesn't hit any mibs out of the smaller circle, the turn is over.

4. The next player shoots at the mibs in the smaller circle or at the other shooters. If the shooter hits another shooter, the player takes one marble from the shooter's owner. Then the player goes again. This shooter, however, may not strike the same player's shooter again.

5. The game ends when there are no mibs left. The player with the most mibs wins.

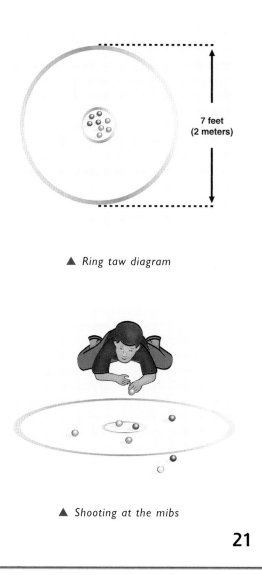

7 feet
(2 meters)

▲ Ring taw diagram

▲ Shooting at the mibs

21

Nucks—A Game from Australia

Nucks is a marble game played in Australia. Players dig holes in the dirt outside. Or they play inside using a cup or shoe as the hole.

Number of players: Two or more

Setup: Dig three shallow holes. Draw a taw line on the ground 10 feet (3 meters) from the first hole.

How to shoot: However you choose

Object: To be the first to hit your marble into the holes in the correct order

How to play:

1. Players number the holes 1, 2, and 3. Then, they decide how the holes must be hit. For example, you might hit your shooter into holes 1, 2, and 3 twice in a row. You can make new rules each game.

2. Players go one at a time. The first player stands behind the taw line. This player tries to get his or her shooter into the first hole. If the player gets his or her shooter into this hole or into the span of this hole, he or she gets to play again. Or, if the player hits someone else's shooter, he or she gets to play again.

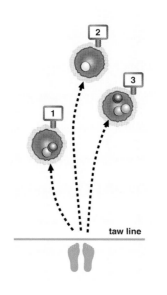

▲ *Number the holes 1, 2, and 3*

3. If the player misses, he or she begins the next turn where his or her shooter landed.

4. The game ends when someone hits the marbles in the holes correctly. The first player to do this is the winner.

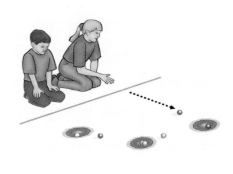

▲ *In nucks, you shoot however you choose.*

23

Kelereng—A Game from Indonesia

Kelereng is a marble game from Indonesia in Southeast Asia. Children usually play this game.

Number of players:	Two or more
Setup:	Draw a square (or triangle) on the ground in an area about 10 by 10 feet (3 by 3 meters). Then draw a taw line 10 feet (3 meters) away.
How to shoot:	Fulking or knuckling down
Object:	To win all the marbles
How to play:	

1. Each player puts the same number of mibs inside the square (or triangle).

2. Players shoot one at a time.

3. Each player stands at the taw line. The player aims his or her shooter at the mibs in the square (or triangle). The player gets all the mibs he or she hits outside the square (or triangle).

4. This player goes again until he or she misses a mib or does not knock a mib out of the square (or triangle). The player leaves his or her shooter where it landed.

5. If a player hits another player's shooter marble, he or she gets all that player's marbles.

6. The game ends when there are no mibs left. The winner gets all the marbles.

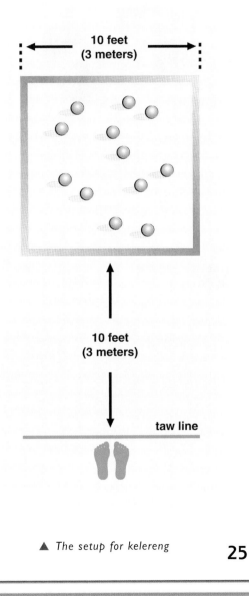

10 feet
(3 meters)

10 feet
(3 meters)

taw line

▲ *The setup for kelereng*

25

Playing and Collecting Marbles

Many marble games are played around the world. Learn as many as you can. The more games you play, the more you will improve.

You may also want to collect marbles. For years, people have collected marbles. Some are very old or colorful. Others may have their own special markings. Marbles may be worth a lot of money. Whether you collect them or play with them, you can have lots of fun with marbles.

▲ *You can see through some marbles.*

Glossary

bombsies—a way to shoot by dropping the shooter marble on the target marble from below eye level

bowling—a way to shoot by throwing the marble underhand or rolling it on the ground

fulking—the most common way to shoot smoothly along the ground. You rest a marble in your curled forefinger and flick your thumb to shoot the marble.

knuckling down—an accurate way to shoot by resting a marble on your curled forefinger, placing your knuckle on the ground, and flicking your thumb

lagging—a shooting game played around the world to decide who is the first player in a marble game

lofting—a way of shooting a marble through the air before it hits the ground

mibs—the target marbles

mibster—a master marble player

shooter—the marble you shoot; also called the shooter marble

span—the distance between your thumb and any other finger on the same hand

span shot—a way to shoot by placing your thumb outside one marble and other finger outside the other marble. You snap your finger and thumb to knock the marbles together.

taw—the shooter marble

taw line—the line you stand behind to shoot your shooter marble, or taw

Did You Know?

- U.S. presidents George Washington, John Quincy Adams, Thomas Jefferson, and Abraham Lincoln played marbles.

- Marbles were most popular from 1920 to 1960.

- The person who gets to play first in marbles is called a ringer.

- When you play marbles, you play for keepsies or friendlies. Keepsies means the players keep all the marbles they win. Friendlies means everyone gets their marbles back at the end of the game.

Want to Know More?

At the Library

Cole, Joanna. *Marbles: 101 Ways to Play.* New York: Morrow Junior Books, 1998.

Editors of Klutz. *The Klutz Book of Marbles.* Palo Alto, Calif.: Klutz, 1989.

Erlbach, Arlene. *Sidewalk Games Around the World.* Brookfield, Conn.: Millbrook Press, 1997.

Gryski, Camilla. *Let's Play: Traditional Games of Childhood.* Buffalo, N.Y.: Kids Can Press, 1998.

Maguire, Jack. *Hopscotch, Hangman, Hot Potato, and Ha, Ha, Ha: A Rulebook of Children's Games.*
New York: Simon and Schuster, 1990.

On the Web

How to Play Marbles

http://web.ukonline.co.uk/conker/conkers-and-ghosts/marbles.htm#championship

For a short history of marbles and information about how to play

Marble Lingo

http://www.marblemansion.com/marble_info/terminology.htm

For a dictionary of different kinds of marbles

The Marble Museum

http://www.marblemuseum.org/

For marble history, pictures, and articles

Through the Mail

Marble Collectors Society of America

P.O. Box 222

Trumbull, CT 06611

To get information about this society and marble shows and exhibits

On the Road

National Marbles Tournament

On the beach in Wildwood, NJ

610/796-1971

To see boys and girls aged fifteen and younger play for national championship titles

Index

About the Author

After graduating from Brown University, Elizabeth Dana Jaffe received her master's degree in early education from Bank Street College of Education. Since then, she has written and edited educational materials. Elizabeth Dana Jaffe lives in New York City.